How To

Make A Living From Property

By

Karen Newton

© Copyright 2012 Karen Newton

First Published in 2005

Revised Edition 2012

Table of Contents

Cover

Legal

Acknowledgments

Preface

What this Book Covers

Intended Market

How the book is structured

About the Author

Authors Comments

Section 1 - Skills & Knowledge

Finding A Suitable Property

Estate Agents

Buying At Auction

BMV (Below Market Value)

Making the Offer

Financing the Deal

Completing the Purchase

Refurbishment

Remortgaging

Cycles

Mentors

Section 1 – Summary

Section 2 – Being A Landlord

Accreditation

Energy Performance Certificates

Gas Safety Certificates

NICEIC

HHSRS

Information Commission Office

Advertising Your Property

Tenant Applications

Guarantors

Referencing

Insurance

Tenancy Agreements

Rents

Bonds and Deposits

Inventories

Property Manuals

HMO

Handling Bad Debts

Section 8 Notices

Section 21 Notices

Applying to Court for Repossession

Court Appointed Bailiff

CCJ

Section 2 Summary

Tiroka Property Management Services

Recommended Reading

Legal

The right of Karen Newton to be identified as Author has been asserted in accordance with the Copyright, Designs and Patent Act 1988

© 2012 Karen Newton.

All rights reserved. No part of this book may be reproduced, stored in a retrieval system, or in any form or by any means, without the prior permission in writing of the author.

Disclaimer: To the fullest extent permitted by law. Karen Newton is providing this written material, its subsidiary elements and its contents on an 'as is' basis and makes no (and expressly disclaim all) representations or warranties of any kind with respect to this written material or it contents including, without limitation, advice and recommendations, warranties or merchantability and fitness for a particular purpose. The information is given for entertainment purpose only – in addition Karen Newton does not represent or warrant that the information accessible via this written material is accurate, complete or current. To the fullest extent permitted by law, Karen Newton or any of her affiliates, partners, employees or other representatives will not be liable for damages arising out of or in connection with the use of this written material. This is a comprehensive limitation of liability that applies to all damages of any kind including (without limitation) compensatory, direct, indirect or consequential damages, loss of date, income or profit, loss of or damage to property and claims of third parties.

Acknowledgments

Thank you to my husband, Ron and daughter, Christina for their continuing support.

Preface

What This Book Covers

This book is a basic introduction to investing in residential property. It provides general information on understanding the world of property investment and dealing with the legal compliances of owning residential properties.

The book encourages the development of your own property portfolio as a basis to becoming a successful investor.

It is hoped that this book can be used as a stepping stone to building your knowledge base for investing.

Intended Market

The book is aimed at the absolute beginner to investing in residential property. While aimed mainly at the British market some of the information provided is readily accessible in many countries just maybe under different names.

How The Book is Structured

This book is split into 2 sections.

Section 1 – deals with the property. It contains information on finding a suitable property, purchasing it and renovating it.

Section 2 – covers the landlord side of property investing. It looks at legal compliances for properties and landlord accreditation.

About The Author

Born in London, raised in South Wales, part educated in France and having lived in New Zealand and Australia, Karen has developed a unique understanding of world economies.

Karen's employment background started in the UK with Inland Revenue where she worked as a clerical assistant on PAYE before moving to Schedule D to specialise in taxes for self-employed and corporations.

Moving to New Zealand Karen went into banking. She worked in various positions within the bank moving to new positions through promotion. Areas covered included Accounting; Teller; International; Training; Visa and Corporate Lending, ISO9000 facilitator. Karen was an Assistant Manager when she left the bank to move into her own business.

During her time in New Zealand she was joint owner of several businesses with her husband as well as individual owner of her own businesses. The businesses included Fire Protection; Security; Electrical Contracting; Air Conditioning. She created history by becoming the first female member of the Fire Protection Contractors Association and went on to become its chairperson, which at the time had a constitutional maximum term of two years. This was amended to allow her to continue in the role for a further five years. In her own right she had a Cosmetic Company and Writing Business

Attending night classes at University in New Zealand Karen studied, Commercial Law; Accounting; Business Management and Quality Management.

Karen developed her interest in writing and wrote advertorials for the local daily newspaper, Hawkes Bay Today; Karting articles for Motorsport NZ and Karting NZ; and numerous articles sold to various magazines.

Returning to the UK in 2000, Karen worked for a recycling consortium as Administrator; Retail Manager and Quality Manager while continuing to build her investment portfolio. Being made redundant twice she eventually retired to concentrate on managing and building her investments.

Today Karen is the owner of several businesses including Property Rentals; Lending; Publishing; Niche Marketing; Mentoring and Network Marketing.

Author's Comments

Everyday there are articles in newspapers about property. Headlines such as 'the property market is about to collapse', 'record property prices', 'first time buyers can't get on the property ladder'. I'm sure you've seen them and read them. As far as the world of newspapers is concerned you only get the downside of property and everything about property is negative. This book has been written to tell you a more balanced view and present some of the positives about investing in property.

When I wrote the first version of this book in 2005 we were in a property boom. Owners of houses in certain parts of the country became property millionaires whether that was their intention or not. Investing in property became a hobby for many as more and more people saw an opportunity to make quick money and then get out of the market.

In September 2007 money started to dry up and we saw queues of people panicking and trying to withdraw their money from Northern Rock Bank. This led on to the Credit Crunch in February 2008. The world of property investing was about to change drastically. Buy to Let mortgages virtually disappeared and have only recently started to come back to the market. Once there used to be over 5000 buy to let mortgages available today there are only a handful of mortgages available for investors.

In the height of the 2000 property boom you could buy a property on day one and by day 10 remortgage it and make £20,000 or £30,000+ profit. Such was the level of finance available and the surge in property prices. Today the property market is subdued. Lenders want you to have owned a property for at least 6 months before you can remortgage.

It is still possible to make money through property but you need to expect to be in the investment for the long term.

Property is still a good investment and despite all the gloom in the newspapers I believe there has never been a better time to invest in property than now. While prices may stagnate for a few years and even decline in some areas of Britain there is no doubt that property prices will again go up.

In the UK we live on an island. There is no land being created however, land is being eroded and at a faster pace as sea levels rise. What land we have is precious. The population expected to reach 70 million by 2050 has been growing 4.5 times faster than predicted. It could very well reach 70 million by 2025. They need somewhere to live. Demand for housing continues to grow with an aging population holding on to their accommodation and younger families desperate to find somewhere to live.

Due to economic times the government main concern is getting government deficit down. Austerity is the new 'buzz' word. Governments are not building houses but rather expecting the private sector to take over not only building new houses but also providing rental accommodation. Residential Social Landlord Associations (RSL) are not getting the funding once received from government to fund new house purchases. They are diversifying into ventures such as property management for the private sector in an attempt to maintain their income.

In April 2013 the new Universal Credit will start and RSL's are expected to have even further reduction in their income. In my region one RSL is expecting its income from LHA (previously housing benefit) to drop from £32 million down to £24 million. That's on top of the government cuts to benefits continually being introduced.

As you can see there will be enormous opportunities for landlords in the private rental sector. As demand increases for housing so will the cost of properties and rents. So as I said previously, there has never been a better time to invest in property.

Section 1

Property

Section 1 - Introduction

Welcome to 'Make A Living From Property' and thank you for purchasing this book. I hope it will provide you with plenty of information and start you on the road to making your fortune through property.

I read many books about making money from property before I started to invest in it. I became frustrated when I realised that many authors hadn't actually invested in property or if they did they only had one or two properties. Their long term plans were to sell the property or properties when they got to retirement age and use the income to buy a pension. A sound plan but it didn't fit in with my plans because the pension provided, while it was possible to live on it, just didn't provide me with the income that I wanted. It wouldn't provide me with the type of lifestyle that I wanted. I also didn't want to wait until retirement age to enjoy the lifestyle.

My plan was and is quite simple. I want an income that allows me to work when I want to work. I want to enjoy the fruits of my labour while I am still young enough and fit enough to be able to enjoy them. If tomorrow I decide I don't want to work again then I don't want to loose my income.

In 1999, I was working in my own business. It was seven days a week, three hundred and sixty five days a year. I had had the business for ten years. During that time I had worked every Christmas day. After 10 years, I had had enough and closed the business deciding there must be a better and easier way.

Today, my life is totally different. I live in a beautiful detached house nestled in 3 acres of land where I grow vegetables and fruit. I own an apartment in the French Alps. While I drive around in my beloved 17 year old battered Jeep I also own a Ferrari 360; Mini Cooper; Mazda RX7 and a Renault Master Van. My daughter goes to private school and when she is on school holidays – 133 days a year – I'm also on holiday.

So how have I achieved this lifestyle?

I achieved it with a very simple plan. I buy an existing property. I renovate the property. Then I find a tenant who wants to rent it. The rent covers my mortgage payments and other compliance costs and pays me a moderate amount of income. Instead of owning just one property I own 60 properties and just keep buying more continually increasing my income.

In twenty years time I will have a mortgage free property portfolio with the full rent being paid to me as my pension. Once the mortgages are paid I will receive almost all the rents as personal income less any taxes. As an example let's say I have a house that is renting for around five hundred pounds a month. That's a conservative figure as today the average rent is £700 per month although this does vary from region to region. But for this example I will use £500 per month. At the moment that pays the mortgage and other compliances but what if the mortgage was repaid. That house would be putting five hundred pounds per month into my pocket. If one property can provide that income what could I do with say ten properties or twenty properties or even more? Imagine thirty properties providing you with five hundred pounds per month income. That is a total income of fifteen thousand pounds a month or one hundred and eighty thousand a year. Best of all, the properties will be growing in value and rentals will be increasing in line with inflation.

Now imagine having more houses. It may seem impossible to start with but it isn't. Even in today's economy where financing is tough there are still several lenders in the buy to let market willing to finance property investment.

In my first year I bought one rental property. The following year I purchased two properties and the year after four properties. I just adjusted the number of properties I purchased to the financing that was available at the time. But it doesn't matter how many properties I own the important thing is that by buying when I could I reaped the benefits of rental income and capital growth. Both of which allowed me to create the lifestyle that I have today.

You too can enjoy any lifestyle you want with only a few short years of effort. This is not a get rich quick scheme. I don't believe there is any such thing unless you are lucky enough to win the lotto. This is a way of securing your future and living the kind of lifestyle you can only dream of.

I hope you enjoy reading this book and start making a living from property and enjoy the lifestyle that it can bring.

Finding A Suitable Property

There are many different types of properties to invest in. Some people choose commercial, some people like apartments while others like new build houses. There are overseas investment properties. As for me, I like existing structurally sound properties needing interior renovation.

My criteria is:

- Existing 2, 3, 4 or 5 bedroom houses
- Structurally sound
- The worst house in the street
- Good opportunity for capital growth
- Good rental opportunities
- Financials Stack Up

Let's look at each item of my criteria in more detail.

1. Existing 2, 3, 4 or 5 bedroom houses

I like existing houses of any size. Two bedroom houses suit either single or married couples. Larger houses cater for couples with children. In most cases I am looking for a tenant that is likely to be more stable. Generally, the more children the more likely the tenant will stay for some time. When apartments are involved frequently the tenant will move around and I like to keep things simple. I don't want to be dealing with new tenants and tenancies every six months.

I like existing properties because they are already built and I know what I am getting. With a 'new build' you are buying off plan. You have to imagine what the property will look like when it is finished. You have to make a down payment which ties up your money until the property is built. This could be months or even years before the property is ready. This is too slow for me. I like to see my return on investment quickly.

Existing houses allows me to assess the neighbourhood to see if it is likely the property will rent quickly. Is it a good neighbourhood, close to schools and shops? Is it a deprived area with unruly behaviour, break in etc. where tenants would prefer not to live.

2. Structurally Sound

When looking at a house I don't care what condition the interior is in. It is quite easy and fairly cheap to put in new kitchens, new bathrooms and repair and decorate the interior. This type of property can be made ready for a tenant to move into within a reasonable time. Reducing the time my property is vacant. On the other hand, if there is damage to a roof or the exterior walls then I don't know how much other damage is involved and this could become quite costly. I would need specialist tradesmen and I would have little or no control on how quickly the work will be done. My aim is to turn a property around very quickly, get it tenanted with the least amount of downtime possible, after all, every day a property is empty it is costing me money instead of making me money.

3. The worst house in the street

One of my first questions is how much are other houses selling for in the street. The property I am looking at normally needs a new kitchen and new bathroom plus general painting and decorating. If house prices in the street are £100,000 and the house is on the market for £95,000 by the time I put in a new kitchen and bathroom I wouldn't make any profit on the property.

I recently purchased a property for £77,000 which came with a separate garage on the other side of the road. Garages were selling for around £6,000 and this one could be quickly sold. Houses in the street were selling for £110,000 to £115,000. I could see a quick capital gain between £33,000 and £44,000.

When I looked at this property I was amazed at how little work I needed to do to get the benefit of the capital gain. The previous owners had started to renovate the property but go into financial difficulty and had to sell. They had started to put in a new kitchen. All the cupboards and fittings were in place it just needed finishing and the flooring needed doing. The lounge and dining rooms were already decorated but there were no doors or door frames. The upstairs was in the same condition. A new bathroom had been started but not finished. A couple of windows needed replacing as the double glazing seals were broken. It looked much worse than it actually was.

I am lucky that my husband and I can do the repair work ourselves. So, we tiled the kitchen floor, refitted and finished the cupboards. Made up the door frames, skirting boards and bought new doors. Replaced the leaky windows, refitted the bathroom suite and carpeted the whole house. Total cost of refurbishment £1500. Time taken to complete the refurbishment was approximately three weeks. The property was then revalued and the house was valued at £115,000 and the garage at £8,000. A capital gain of £46,000 less £1500 for refurbishments, a net gain was achieved of £44,500 for three weeks work.

4. Good Opportunity for Capital Growth

For some reason most people are scared of capital growth. They imagine having to pay tax to the government and that this wipes out their profit. If I was going to sell the property I would probably have similar concerns but my system relies on good capital growth, holding on to the property and finding a tenant.

Using the property mentioned above in section 3, I will give an example of how my system works.

I purchased the property for £77,000. I obtained a buy-to-let mortgage for 85% of the purchase price, £65450 and put down a deposit of £11550. When the property was revalued the total value of the property was £115,000 and £8,000 for the garage which equals £123,000. I then remortgaged the property using another buy-to-let mortgage for 85% of the new value. This time the mortgage was for £104,550. The existing mortgage was repaid and I was left with cash in my hand of £39,100. This money is then mine to with as I choose as long as it is legal. There is no tax to pay on this money. (The Chancellor hasn't yet come up with a way of taxing loan money but I'm sure he's working on it!) I had enough money to put a deposit on two more properties plus pay myself an income for the three weeks work on the property. There is no capital gains tax to pay because I still own the property. And now I have a tenant in the property paying rent which covers the cost of the mortgage repayments. Plus that property has just provided me with the deposits to purchase another two properties.

5. **Good Rental Opportunities**

When looking for a property I like to be sure I will get good rentals for it. So, I tend to look at the area. I am looking for properties which are modern. Most of my houses are less than forty years old. I find the more modern type houses rent much better than the older style houses. But that is only my opinion with the area I work in. It might be the reverse in another region. The house needs to be in a fairly good location. I am looking for areas where the properties are mainly owner/occupied. These areas are generally better maintained, gardens look better and the overall impression can add a few more thousand pounds to the property when it has been refurbished and revalued. The other criteria I am looking for is local amenities. That is how close is the school, the bus stop, the shopping centre or the local store. All these things make the property more attractive to rent and I can ask higher rents for them.

6. Finances Stack Up

By finances stack up I am talking about the costs for maintaining the property, compliances and mortgage repayments. The property also needs to provide me with a reasonable return.

In today's market with cheaper finance it is easier to balance the budget but what happens when mortgage rates go up which inevitably they will do. It might be five or ten years before they go up but you need to ensure you can weather any increases in the cost of finance.

If I borrow £100,000 at 3.99% then monthly repayments based on interest only will be £332.50 if interest rates go up to 5% repayments will be £416.66. Rents in my area for 3 bedroom house are circa £550. If interest rates are 5% I would have monthly net income of £550 - £416.66 = £133.34 per month. From this I have to pay insurance, roughly £10 per month, and gas compliances of £40 per year of £3.33. My profit is about £120 a month. If mortgages go above 5% I would still have a reasonable margin to be able to absorb the increase without getting into financial difficulty.

I have property in another region where rents are only £325 a month for a 3 bedroom house. As you can see the figures do not add up and the purchase is not viable. If I purchased a property in this region with a £100,000 mortgage I would be losing money every month and would quickly become bankrupt. Our aim is to make money not lose it.

Estate Agents

Love them or loathe them if you are looking at investing in property there is every possibility that you will have to deal with Estate Agents.

Building a relationship with an Estate Agent can be very beneficial. I have two local agents who telephone me immediately a property becomes available that they think will meet my criteria. They have got to know me over the years and know what I am looking for. I generally get to view a property before it goes on public release. Sometimes getting in early allows me to get the property at a good price. It very much depends on how willing the vendor is to sell.

While I have purchased properties from many other Estate Agents some are very difficult to build any relationship with. As a result most of my purchases come from the two agents I have the relationship with.

The relationship is two-way in that they save me a lot of time searching for property. They know that when I make an offer if it is accepted that the sale will go through. This means they can recommend to their customer that my offer be accepted knowing that I have a good track record with them and no difficulty in funding the purchase. I save them time in finding would be purchasers and showing the properties. They get their commissions quickly and for little work and are free to concentrate on the more difficult houses to sell.

Buying At Auction

A popular way to buy is at auction. An online search will tell you what auctions are being held in your area. Prices depend very much on what the market is doing. Don't assume auction is the best way to buy.

Before going to auction do your research. Information packs are available and your solicitor can verify everything is okay prior to the auction date. It is also important to have finance in place for your purchase. Settlement on auction property sales is 28 days. Most lenders take longer than that to process loans. If your funds are not in place before the bidding starts ensure you have enough personal money to cover the costs. Penalties are steep if you fail to complete the purchase by the deadline.

While many people will swear auctions are the best way to buy, I have only ever purchased one property at auction and that was a cash purchase, or rather, I had sufficient money on my credit cards to make the purchase.

Do your homework on any property you are considering bidding on. To obtain a mortgage the property must have at the least a sink in the kitchen. You'll be surprised how many auction properties need a lot of work and don't have a sink. Visit the property and look at the condition for yourself.

Good deals can be found at auction but it is very easy for things to turn sour quickly. I remember a person asking me about a property he wanted to buy at auction. It was an old hotel that could be easily converted into apartments. It sounded a good deal provided he was able to buy it at a certain price. My first question was did he have finance in place to which he replied yes. He went to auction and bought the property. He contacted me about two months later as he still had not completed on the deal even though it was suppose to be done within 28 days. When I asked about his finance he said his broker had been unable to get a lender to look at the deal and was still trying. I put him in contact with my broker. The original finance never existed and was only the word of a financial broker telling him he should be able to get a mortgage. It took four months to get finance in place and he paid a considerable sum in penalties for not completing within the 28 days. Don't fall into the same trap. Make sure you have a lender and finance in position before bidding.

When at the auction make sure you stick to your budget. If the property goes above the price you think it should go for don't get carried away in the bidding process. Stick to your price and walk away from the deal if it goes to a higher price. There are plenty more out there.

An aquaintance of mine buys a lot of property at auction but hides his identity. He has found if it is known he is bidding on a property the price goes up very quickly. The assumption is if he is interested in the property then it must be a good one so all the inexperienced bidders in the room start bidding wildly forcing the price up. Don't get into that trap. Make your own decisions on which properties you want, set a maximum price and don't go over it.

Auctions can provide some cheap properties but you need to do your homework. Remember there are alternative ways to buy properties.

BMV (Below Market Value)

The process involves finding someone who wants to sell their property and rent it back. It seems to be a very popular way to buy properties by the adverts I continually see in the papers.

Usually, the seller has financial difficulties and is desperate to sell. The vendor is usually in default on a mortgage. The buyer makes an offer below the market value for the property but with sufficient to cover repaying the mortgage. The seller then stays in the house as the new tenant.

This works quite well for many investors as you the investor has bought a cheap property and has a ready made tenant who because it was their own home generally will continue to look after the property as though they still live in it.

One problem to be careful about is that some lenders won't lend for this type of deal as they require the vendor to have vacant possession before releasing the funds. There are ways around this but you need a flexible understanding lawyer to do this.

Making The Offer

Okay, so now you have found the ideal property, the next step is to make an offer on the property.

Buyer or Seller's Market

One of the first things you need to decide is if it is a buyer's or a seller's market. I first started buying property in 2001 and house prices were starting to rise. There were still the occasional opportunities to negotiate on price but not many. For the next couple of years prices continued to rise. During this time there were a lot of people interested in buying property. If you tried to negotiate on price it was declined and the next buyer was waiting in the wings to purchase the property at the seller's price. This is what is known as a seller's market. During this period if I decided I wanted a property I would offer the price the seller was asking.

Since the credit crunch of 2008 we are in a buyers market. We have a lot of properties coming onto the market and unfortunately some of those are properties are about to become repossessions. What is happening at the moment is many homeowners have mortgages that were on fixed rate loans and then reverted to the lenders Standard Variable Rate (SVR). Despite cheaper funding being available these lender have introduced an annual increase in their SVR rate.

Some homeowners now find themselves with mortgage rates of 7% or more and are unable to remortgage as property prices have dropped and they have negative equity. The mortgages have fallen into arrears due to the high interest rates and people losing their jobs. The problem they now face is that they must get the highest price possible for their property because if they don't sell the house high enough they will still end up owing the mortgage company money. So frequently these sellers can't move on price. They still need a quick sale and so the property is already listed for the minimum price the vendor can afford to sell at.

If you have your mind set on a particular property, it is still worth trying a lower figure but don't be disappointed if it is declined. Decide what your maximum offer will be. Make a lower offer and keep increasing your offers until you reach your maximum. If you still don't get an offer accepted walk away. Move on to the next property. There is always a good deal out there. Don't be afraid that it is too good an offer to walk away from. There is no such thing. I find there is a good deal to be made every day. You just have to keep looking.

Don't be afraid to put in a low offer. I saw a property listed for £85,000. I purchased the property for £75,000. My first offer was accepted. I keep wondering what could have been the lowest possible price on this property.

I am sometimes disappointed when my first offer is accepted as I like to feel that I have worked for the deal. I also wonder how much cheaper I could have purchased the property for. But, you don't want to get greedy. You are working on a win/win situation. You get a price that you are happy to purchase the property and the seller gets a price they are happy to sell at.

Special Deals

There are special deals that can be negotiated such as shared ownership, stamp duty being paid, discount or a percentage of the deposit being paid. The only ones I have used are a percentage or all of the deposit being paid which I will now explain.

In 2001, my husband and I bought our first house. Although our plan was to eventually make the property into a rental property our main aim at the time was to provide us with somewhere to live. We found a house which matched our rental property criteria. It was a three bedroom end terraced structurally sound property. The owner had died five years earlier and the son and daughter had jointly inherited the house but hadn't done anything with it. The property was listed with the estate agent for £54,000.

Before searching for a property we had been to our bank and they had indicated the maximum amount they would lend us and it was to be no more than 95% of the purchase price. This property fell within the criteria but we couldn't come up with the 5% deposit of £2700. So we asked the vendor to gift us the 5% deposit. They declined. We walked away from the deal.

A few weeks later we were walking around the Estate Agents and saw the price had been reduced on the property. So we put in another offer, asking again for the 5% deposit and again we were declined.

About 3 months later we saw the price of the property had again been reduced and this time the asking price was £42,000 plus the vendor was offering a 5% deposit. We jumped in immediately and did the deal. So in fact, we bought the house for £39,900. All it cost us was time, patience and £300 in legal fees. We borrowed the

£300 on our credit card. We lived in the house for a few years and remortgaged it a couple of times releasing equity which enabled us to buy a few more rental properties. When we were ready to move it became a rental property.

Making the Offer

This is the easy part. Tell the Estate Agent how much you want to offer. They contact the seller with your offer and then let you know if it has been accepted or not. If not, decide if you want to make another offer immediately or wait a while or even walk away from the deal. If your offer is accepted the Estate Agent will send a memorandum of sale to you, the seller and both parties solicitors.

Financing The Deal

Since the credit crunch in 2008 finding the finance to purchase your first property can be more difficult. But don't let it put you off. There are lenders out there waiting to lend money and they have different types of loans to suit your needs even if you have CCJ's there are still companies out there prepared to lend to you.

Over the past year some of the familiar buy to let lenders have started coming back into the market. Paragon and Kensington were some of the big companies that lent to people with adverse credit. The fact that they are back in the market means the buy to let market is starting to free up again.

Some of the building societies are also starting to lend to buy to let again.

The Deposit

If you are lucky then you will already have a deposit saved. If not a few suggestions are:

1. If you are currently renting your home you could do as I described in the previous chapter and purchase a house for you to live in with a gifted

deposit. As long as the property has opportunity for capital growth you can do the work to it while you live in it. Remortgage to the new value and raise the deposit for your rental property.

A word of caution – don't say you are going to live in the property and then not live there. This is obtaining money fraudulently and you could end up with a jail term. There is no need to acquire money fraudulently as there are numerous lenders who will lend to you legally. If you decide you don't want to live in the property ask the lender if they will change the mortgage to a buy-to-let. Some lenders will do so and charge a small fee for doing it.

2. The government have schemes to help first time buyers get onto the property ladder. You could start by using one of these schemes and stay in the property for a while. Once you are a home owner it is surprising what other money becomes available.

3. If you already own your house then you may be able to remortgage it and raise the deposit from the equity in your home.

4. You can raise a personal loan and use the money for the deposit

5. You can raise the money on your credit cards. This is a trick I use on some purchases. I have several credit cards on which I can drawdown cash. The cash is used to purchase the property. When the work has been done on the property and a mortgage is in place the cash is used to repay the credit cards. The only problem with this system is if it takes 6 months to get a mortgage on your property the credit card costs can be very expensive so you need to have finance in place quickly to reduce your costs of funding your purchase this way.

6. Ask friends or family if they can help

7. What do you have that you can sell? It is amazing what can be sold and bought on ebay. What seems like junk to you can be a must have item for someone else.

The Mortgage

When it comes to getting an actual mortgage I would highly recommend you use a mortgage broker. With the mortgage market being so restricted at present a good broker will know where to get a mortgage to suit your current financial situation.

Finding a suitable broker is the tricky part. My husband and I have separate property portfolios. Between us we have tried several brokers. There have been brokers who charged fees up front and some who didn't. We now have a fantastic broker who has made such a big difference to our business. It really does pay to shop around. Don't be afraid to sack someone if they don't perform to your expectations. You want someone that you can get on well with. Someone you trust implicitly and someone who is prepared to work hard on your behalf. After all, you will hopefully be putting a lot of work their way.

Different Types of Mortgages

We use different types of mortgages and there are so many out there I won't go into all of them here. The storage space on my computer probably isn't large enough, so I'll just cover a few that we use.

- **Interest Only** – the monthly interest charges are the lowest possible and allow me to purchase or remortgage at slightly higher levels than a standard mortgage would. Many lenders are moving away from this type of mortgage and several have in recent months withdrawn this type of mortgage from the market.
- **Interest only discounted** – this mortgage is interest only repayments but the initial payments are at a discounted rate. For example, I have some mortgages which have a discount of 0.25% below the normal rate fixed for two years. In other words for the first two years of the mortgage instead of paying the normal rate of 5.90% I am paying interest at 5.65%. If rates go up or down then the rate I am paying will move in the same direction.
- **Interest only fixed** – again this mortgage is interest only but the initial period of the loan is at a fixed rate before moving to a variable rate. With this type of loan I have some mortgages fixed at 2.99% for two years before reverting to the standard interest rate. If rates go up or

down the payments remain the same until the fixed period ends.

Generally, I try to purchase the property on an interest only variable rate loan with no tie-ins. (by tie-ins I mean that I can repay the mortgage at any time without any penalties) Once I have completed the refurbishment I then remortgage again on interest only but at the best deal available on the day. At this stage it doesn't matter if I am tied in to a mortgage for two years as I have got out of the property the capital growth I was after and have sufficient money to purchase my next property or two plus pay myself an income. If the mortgage is fixed for two years then I have the added security of knowing my payments won't alter during that period.

Insurance

Most broker will have a list of insurance companies who offer buy-to-let buildings insurance. This will need to be in place before exchanging contracts.

Completing The Purchase

So far you have found a property that you like, you have obtained finance and insurance. The next part is to let your solicitor do the rest of the work. Their job is to check the property is okay to purchase. They do this through various searches. Once happy they will agree a contract, exchange of contract date and a completion date. Once all the terms have been agreed and you have paid the deposit you and the vendor will sign and exchange contracts.

Once the contract has been exchanged you must have insurance in place for the property. You will become the owner on the date that has been agreed for completion. If for some reason completion doesn't take place and it is yours or your solicitors fault you will be liable for breach of contract fees. So make sure you both have everything in place to complete the sale on the agreed date before exchanging contracts.

Solicitors

Solicitors are a personal choice and finding a good one can be difficult. Between my husband and I we have sacked five solicitors before finding one who worked the way we wanted and within a timeframe. With some solicitors conveyancing (buying and selling houses) is a very small part of their business and you may find yourself at the bottom of their priority list.

My husband once put together a deal to purchase five houses at once from a landlord who was moving out of residential property and into commercial property. The vendor wanted a quick sale as he needed the money for another deal. All our finance was in place and we were waiting on the solicitor. The solicitor knew the urgency and drew down the mortgage funds immediately but then got sidetracked with other work. My husband started visiting the office every day to find out why nothing was happening. Three month later we still did not have any of the properties and we were making repayments on mortgages for properties we didn't own. The vendor became irate because he couldn't complete on his deal. Eventually, the whole deal fell through and we were out of pocket for 3 months mortgage payments. All because the solicitor had more important work and needless to say he didn't work for us again.

I can't emphasise how important a good solicitor is. Part of this business is building a team of good people around you. It takes time to find those people but once you have them magic starts to happen and your business will grow exponentially.

Refurbishment

Well congratulations, you are now the proud owner of a run down property that needs renovating. The question is where to start. This is where many people make or lose money. They get so hung up on everything being so perfect and designing their ideal house they forget this is a rental property.

There are obviously things that need to be done to the property but essentially this is a rental property and the needs are basic. A house needs a kitchen, a bathroom, and tidy clean rooms.

The important areas for increasing the value of the property are the kitchen and bathroom. The trick is to make it look like you have spent a lot of money on the property without doing so. You want a valuer to like what they see and at the same time you want a tenant to fall in love with the place. So detailed in this section are the steps I go through with a renovation. Now, I'm lucky because I can do some of the renovations myself with assistance from my husband and this DIY approach does keep the cost down. If you need to get someone in you will have to allow for the labour costs when calculating overall spending.

The Kitchen

- Use tiles on the floor. These can be the cheapest possible from any DIY store. I tend to use the stores own brand which are cheapest to buy. Bulk deals can also help reduce the cost.
- Build a base for the units to sit on and tile up the front of the base. Cheaper than buying facing boards to match door fronts and tiles tend to last longer.
- Units – stick to one particular brand. It makes it easier to mix and match at other properties especially when there are deals on.
- Door and draw fronts – check which ones are on special. It reduces your costs. Personally, I tend to stick to B&Q and at their stores there is usually one style on special each month.
- Sinks and taps – I shop around for the best deal on the day.
- Bench tops – again I shop around for the best deal on the day. I like to buy formica sheets that match the bench tops and this forms the wall backing between the base units and wall units. Depending on price tiling can be more cost effective if there are specials on.

- I use wall fitted ovens and hobs to add the finishing touches. Again shop around for the best deal.
- Paint the ceilings and remaining walls. Usually white and magnolia are the standard colours.

The kitchen is now complete and my average cost to renovate a kitchen is seven hundred and fifty pounds.

I purchased a property for £84,000. The property was in good condition and only needed the kitchen renovating. It took two weeks to complete the renovations at a cost of £750. Once finished the property was revalued at £110,000. I was able to get a new mortgage for £93500

So the figures for this property look like this.

New Mortgage	£93500
Less the original Mortgage	£71400
Less the cost of the kitchen	£ 750
Total Profit	£21350

Enough profit to provide the deposit for another property and still have some left over to pay my wages for the time spent on renovating the kitchen.

Bathroom

The next important room for adding value to the property is the bathroom. Again it is surprising how cheaply a DIY bathroom can be done that looks terrific and adds value to the property.

Bathroom suite – can be purchased for around £199 from DIY stores such as B&Q. Look for the specials there are always plenty around. The suite will include bath, toilet, hand basin and all the taps and fittings needed.

Walls – tile around the bath area only and paint the remainder of the walls. But if you want to install a shower tile the whole area exposed to water.

Floors – Tile or Bathroom Carpet can be used on the floor and looks very good.

Again my budget is around £750 for the bathroom it doesn't include labour which my husband and I provide to reduce costs.

I purchased a property for £69950. It was already a rental property but the landlord was moving on to commercial property and wanting to sell. A new kitchen had already been done by the vendor all I had to do was a new bathroom and carpet in the lounge area. Once the bathroom and carpet were done the property was revalued at £110,000.

The figures for the property were:

New Mortgage	£93500 (85% of £110,000)
Repay old Mortgage	£59458
Bathroom renovation	£ 350
Carpet	£ 400
Profit	£33292

With the profit on this property I was able to set aside £30,000 as a deposit on another two properties and the balance was kept for wages and materials on other projects.

Decorating

The general rule of thumb when it comes to decorating a property is to always decorate it the same way - white ceilings, white woodwork, white doors and magnolia on the walls. For carpet I stick to plain colours and the same colour throughout the house. As for the colour it depends on my supplier and what special deals he is willing to do on the day.

If you can build a relationship with a local supplier you will be surprised at how good a discount you can get once they know you will keep coming back and giving them more work.

I purchased a property for £75,000. It had a new kitchen which needed finishing touches such as skirting boards and door frames but the bulk of the work had been done. There was a tiled floor and new units and sink. The bathroom unit was good but the bathroom needed decorating. The rest of the house also needed decorating. For two weeks work the house was redecorated and new carpet laid. When the property was revalued it came in at £123,000.

The figures for this property were:

New Mortgage   £104550 (85% of £123,000)

Repay old mortgage   £ 63750

Renovation Costs   £   900

Profit   £39900

Again there was sufficient profit to be able to put a deposit on another two property purchases and have sufficient left to cover wages and renovation costs on the next projects.

From the examples on the previous pages you can see the potential for profits by using the criteria discussed in previous sections of the book. The structure is sound so only internal work is required. The property is the worst in the street so it can be brought up to street value with some TLC. This provides the capital and the cashflow to move forward onto other projects.

By giving you several examples you can see this is not a case of finding the one unique property that no one else will discover for a hundred years. There is a good deal to be find everyday just by looking in the right place.

Suppliers

One of the things I have found is that by sticking to the same suppliers I get a good discount. The suppliers know me well and know I will be back time and time again.

In any business, what is known as repeat business, is a very valuable commodity and worth paying for with good discounts. What I mean is that it is cheaper to keep an existing customer and look after them ensuring they come back to you again and again than it is to advertise and try to attract new customers to your business.

If the suppliers you are dealing with don't look after you then look else where until you find a good supplier worth supporting.

Remortgaging

The secret to being able to buy more than one property is remortgaging.

So far you have purchased a property, renovated it and now you want to buy some more properties and pay yourself for the work you have done by releasing the equity in the property. This is done through a remortgage.

These days being able to remortgage is a little more difficult and you may have to hold on to the property for 6 months before doing so. The mortgage market is changing every day and your mortgage broker is the best person to advise you on how to progress from here.

In my case I now pay cash for my properties. I still have to own the property for a while before I can put a mortgage on it but the process is quicker than mortgaging and then remortgaging.

Whether or not I am putting a mortgage on a property for the first time or remortgaging the property I still go through the same process and make sure I have as much evidence as possible to support the value I'm claiming on the property and the mortgage I am asking for.

My process is:

1. Have a look around all the Real Estate Agents and find properties for sale in the street the property is in and nearby streets. Always pick up a flyer. You need to know the condition the property is in and the photos on the flyer will give you an idea. Keep flyers for future reference.
2. Register with Land Registry so you can check the actual sales price achieved on properties. Rightmove website can also provide some of this information. If you have been visiting the Estate Agents for a few months and kept the flyers you can compare how much the property was listed for and how much it eventually sold for. It might be a property was on the market for £100,000 but sold for £85,000. The valuer will be looking at actual sales not the marketed price. This comparison will also help you with buying future properties.
3. Complete a new mortgage application with your mortgage broker. Your broker should be able to find a few loans that meet your criteria. You are

wanting the cheapest possible interest rate with a fixed rate for as long a period as possible. There are deals available at present where you can get a fixed interest rate for 5 years.
4. Once the application has been approved I meet the valuer at the property and show him the evidence to support the new value I am looking for on the property. I have built up a good relationship with some valuers and they will take the information offered. The also know I haven't just plucked any old figure out of the sky but that I have done my research and am being realistic with the valuation I am expecting. Other valuers will refuse anything you try to offer. Don't let them unnerve you.
5. I wait for the mortgage broker to get back to me and confirm the application has been approved or let him tell me any problems that have come up and how we go about resolving them.
6. Once I have a confirmed offer I then let the solicitor do his job. While I am waiting for the remortgage to go through I am looking for my next property deal.

Valuers

One of the drawbacks of this business is that you are at the mercy of the valuer. Most of them are good and fair with their property values. However, there are some who will deliberately mark a property down in value because it is a rental property. There is one such valuer in my area and basically if he rings to do the valuation I tell him I am not interested. I then go back to my mortgage broker and tell him that I have refused to use this valuer. Normally, the lender will send out another valuer. If they won't then I simply take out a mortgage with another company.

General Information

When you invest in property or any other investment opportunity it helps to understand cycles.

Cycles

The financial world works in cycles. The best way to imagine a cycle is like a circle. At the top of the circle is the high for the investment. At the bottom of the circle is the low for the investment. The left and right hand sides of the circle tell you if are in an upward or downward cycle and helps provide a focal point of where you are. The trick to investing is getting into the investment at the bottom of the circle and getting out at the top of the circle. The problem being that no one knows when the investment is at a high or when it is at the low.

I came back to the UK in 2000. At that time in my area of South Wales you could purchase a nice 3 bedroom house for £30,000. House prices were steadily rising and by 2007 the same house was selling for £115,000. Today house prices are going down and the house is worth about £90,000. Will it go back down to £30,000 unlikely but you never know.

If you had purchased the house for £30,000 and sold for £115,000 you would be very pleased with the profit you had made. You bought at the low of the cycle and sold at the high.

The story would be totally different if you bought at the high of £115,000 and were now wanting to sell at today's price of £90,000. It would be a loss and you would not be very happy with the result. Unfortunately, this is a situation many property owners find themselves in at present. The value of their houses has dropped to below the price they purchased the property for and due to the size of the mortgage they have they find themselves in negative equity. There are many property owners now waiting for house prices to go up so they can sell.

There are different cycles for different investments. Take Gold as another example, as I rewrite this book it is still climbing in value. If you had purchased Gold at $400 USD and it is currently at $1700 USD you would be pleased with your investment. The big question is 'Has Gold reached the cycle high yet?' Nobody knows the answer to that. We all like to think we have a crystal ball and can predict the rise and falls but we don't and we just do the best we can.

I keep my own cycle information in a simple excel spread sheet. I use the information to help make a decision on whether to buy or sell. I don't base it solely on the cycle but it does help as part of my overall criteria for an investment.

Each month Land Registry release actual sales figures for properties registered the month before. It is very easy when looking at the current month's figures to say property has gone up or down. If however, if you keep your own information and plot on a graph the sales figures you can see immediately if this is just a blip in the figures or a definite trend.

Cycles can be a very handy tool but don't get hung up on them as they only tell part of the story.

Mentors

The Karen Newton Mentoring Program

In 1999 I read Rich Dad, Poor Dad by Robert Kiyosaki and got very excited about the possibilities and opportunities explained in the book. In early 2000, we were living in New Zealand and my husband and I travelled for five and a half hours from our home town to Auckland to hear Robert Kiyosaki speak and then travelled home again. Eleven hours spent travelling to listen to a speech that lasted about 2 hours.

On the way home my husband and I talked non-stop about the possibilities that were presented to us. We were so excited we took another day off from our business to read Robert's new book 'Rich Dad's Guide to Investing'. By the end of the day we had a plan.

We tried to implement the plan but it didn't go as we had hoped. New Zealand has a very high home ownership and when we talked to lenders about borrowing for rental properties we received resounding no after no. We then decided our plan would work better in Australia. They have a much larger population and higher rental market. We packed up and moved to

Australia. Again things did not go according to our plan. We had been in Australia for only a couple of days when my mother who lived in the UK died. We travelled to Britain. The next eight months were taken up with hospital visits and funerals as I lost six family members.

During this time I got a job and so did my husband. We still talked about our plans and are evenings were filled with walks around the town centre looking at property for sale in every real estate agents office. On weekends we would visit the offices, talk about wanting to build a property portfolio and pick the brains of any agent willing to give us a few minutes of their time.

We talked to bank managers who sadly all said 'forget it'.

But we persevered and one year later bought our first property. It wasn't a rental but a home for us to live in. Three months later we bought our first rental property. Then we got side tracked. We were both working and had little or no time to work on our plan. We finally, came to realise our plan was the most important thing to us. Nothing was going to stop us achieving it. So my husband gave up his job to concentrate on building a rental portfolio full time. I worked on the other aspects of the plan in my free time. Within 3 years I was able to leave the job I had and work full-time on our plan.

Lucky for us both my husband and I were able to motivate and support each other and have the mutual determination to make our plan work. Many people don't have someone encouraging them along the way and eventually they give up.

For this reason, I run a 12 month mentoring program. I guarantee at the end of the 12 months you will be wealthier and have better income than when you started on my program provided you are willing to put in the effort needed.

From day one I will help you identify where you are currently with your finances, the areas that need to be worked on and introduce you to your first strategic step towards financial independence. At the end of the 12 months you will have gained substantial knowledge and be wealthier and have better cashflow. You will have direct contact with me via email and telephone as well as a monthly one on one meeting.

I will help you put together a plan that identifies what you want to achieve. Then I will act as your mentor and coach. I'll be there to keep you on track with your plan for 12 months by which time you will have learned and earned enough that your successes should be enough motivation to keep you going.

You can get further information by emailing me info@karennewton.co.uk please put mentor in the subject line.

After 12 months the support doesn't stop. We just move into a different stratosphere where you can join our elite club and get exposure to larger and more sophisticated investment opportunities.

Everyone needs a mentor whether a personal mentor to keep them on track or mentoring through books, dvd's, workshops and seminars. The more support you have the greater your successes will come.

Section 1 - Summary

When you are looking at buying a rental property it is a good practice to have a set criteria that you can work within as not all properties a suitable for renting.

Building a team around you is important and makes the whole process run smoothly. If you have a good solicitor and good mortgage broker they will work together to make sure the sale goes through as quick as possible.

When it comes to the renovation of the property keep it simple. It needs to be compliant with Health and Safety Regulations but does not need to be expensive to refurbish. Have a good team and set yourself a time frame for completing the work. In my properties work is completed within 3 or 4 weeks. I normally have a tenant waiting to move in once it has been completed. This ensures mortgage payments are covered and you are not having to fund an empty property for months on end.

Section 2

Landlords

Section 2 – Introduction

So now you have a property that has been refurbished and is ready to let or so you think. In this next section we will look at the legal requirements before you can let your property. We also take a look at how you go about finding a tenant. And the processes needed in the running of your property investment business.

Accreditation

Accreditation as a landlord is becoming more important. Some councils in Wales are insisting that if you want to let a property then you need to be accredited. While no restriction is in place with other councils it is likely that this is the start of moving to all landlords eventually becoming accredited in the near future.

What's Involved in Becoming Accredited?

National Landlord Association Accreditation Scheme

The National Landlord's Association run their own accreditation system. This involves learning online material from their library and attending training course and forums.

Accreditation is earned once you have accrued a certain number of points which you gain from attending courses, forums and using the resources in the National Landlords Association Library. Then each year you need to continue earning the points to show you are continually learning and developing your knowledge and skills.

You can also obtain accreditation by co-opting your accreditation from another scheme.

Further information can be found at the National Landlord's Association website.

http://www.landlords.org.uk

Landlord Accreditation Wales (LAW)

In Wales it is compulsory to attend a one training course and pass a written test to get the initially accreditation. There after you need to attend further courses, forums and use other learning systems to prove you are continuing to develop your knowledge and skills.

Again points are awarded for attendance at the courses and forums. Provided you earn enough points each year your accreditation continues.

Further information can be found at Landlord Accreditation Wales website.

http://www.welshlandlords.org.uk/

Once you are accredited Landlord Accreditation Wales provides you with digital certificates and logos which they encourage you to use to show you are a professional landlord. It also helps them build awareness of their brand.

Below is a sample of a digital logo.

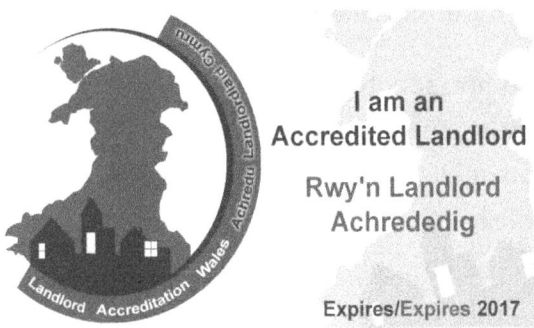

Benefits of Accreditation

1. Some Councils in Wales are insisting landlords are accredited before they are allowed to make a property available to rent. It is thought this is the first step towards licensing all landlords. Currently

only landlords who operate HMO (housing of multiple occupation – covered in a later section of this book) are required to be registered before they can let their property.
2. The Councils and Landlord Accreditation Wales allow accredited landlords to advertise properties to let through their website.
3. Councils will provide prospective tenants with a list of landlords operating in their region. The list only contains accredited landlords. Both the list and the websites provide you the landlord with free advertising for your property.
4. Some Councils are actively sourcing suppliers who will give better discounts to landlords who are accredited.

Energy Performance Certificates (EPC)

Before any house can be put up for sale or rent it needs to have an Energy Performance Certificate (EPC) similar to the one shown below.

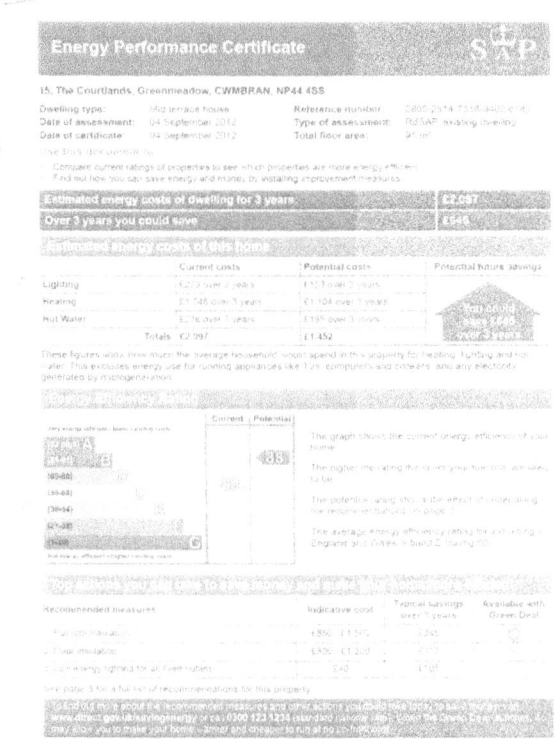

If landlords do not obtain an EPC they can be find £5,000.

In January 2013 the government is introducing a scheme called Green Deal. The scheme allows any landlord/tenant to borrow money to improve the efficiency of the property. The cost of repaying the loan is offset against gas and electricity bills. It is then intended that by 2015/16 the government will introduce legal requirements that, if a property has an E rating or lower the landlord will not be allowed to let the property until energy savings measures have been installed and the EPC rating has increased to a D or higher.

The types of installations covered under Green Deal are:

- Cavity Wall Insulation
- Loft Insulation
- Floor Insulation
- Solar Panels and other electricity renewal systems
- Low Energy Light Bulbs
- Jacket Insulation for hot water tanks
- Condensating Boilers

Most of the above measures are available through the Green Deal Scheme along with many other energy efficient systems.

Repayment of Green Deal Loans

All money borrowed under the Green Deal is to be repaid. Under Green Deal loan repayments are to be made through electricity bills. The idea being that your bills will remain the same and the money saved through the energy efficient savings will be used to repay the loan. Electricity bills are not allowed to go up to repay the loan.

If a tenant applies for the Green Deal Loan it has to also be approved by the Landlord. When a tenant moves the repayment of the loan stays with the house.

Gas Safety Certificates

Before a tenant moves into a property and annually thereafter, the Landlord must have in place a Gas Safety Certificate. See example below.

It is a legal requirement for a gas safety certificate to be in place on all properties that are let. If landlord's fail to have one in place they can be fined hefty sums and/or given a jail sentence.

The inspection must be done by a Gas Safety Engineer and a list of those engineers can be found at http://www.gassaferegister.co.uk/

Anyone who is on the register usually displays the following logo. But don't accept the logo as evidence they are approved. Check the register at the above website.

Remember it is your neck on the line if you don't have a current gas safety or an invalid gas safety.

NICEIC

The NICEIC is an electrical certificate for the property and is valid for 5 years.

Currently it is not compulsory to have an electrical certificate. But it does give peace of mind knowing your property has been checked and verified safe.

Under current legislation all landlords must do an annual check of power points, lights switches etc. to ensure they are safe.

It is recommended that PAT tests be done on any electrical appliance in the property as a safe guard. It is not compulsory as this only applies to commercial at present. However, if you have electric ovens or hobs, fridges, freezers, washing machines, dishwashers that form part of your property having a PAT test says the appliances are in a fit state for your rental property.

An example of an NICEIC report is shown below.

And the logo to look for is below. Again don't assume that the person is approved because they are displaying the logo. Check and ensure they are registered.

As with any registration the tradesman is required to ensure he is up to date with latest legislation and this means sitting tests on a regular basis. So don't be afraid to check if their registration is still current.

HHSRS

The Housing Health and Safety Rating System (HHSRS) is a risk based system used by local authorities to assess the potential risk or harm in any residential property. It was introduced under the Housing Act 2004 and came into effect on 6 April 2006 and applies to residential properties in England and Wales.

The main principal of the system is any residential premises should provide a safe and healthy environment for any potential occupier or visitor to the property.

Councils are empowered to ensure properties in the private rented sector comply with HHSRS. They do this by assessing whether properties have housing hazards of which there 29 different classifications.

The council have the power to inspect any rented property and perform a risk assessment -this looks at the likelihood of an incident arising from the condition of the property and the likely harmful outcome. For example, how likely is a fire to break out, what will happen if one does?

Where the council inspector identifies risks in the first instance they are advised [within the legislation guidance], to try to work with the Landlord on an informal basis to resolve such issues.

Landlords must work with the council and demonstrate they are trying to resolve the issue. If the landlord fails to co-operate the council can charge for visits, enforcement and any work they themselves contract on the property to rectify the risk.

The Council have the right to serve notice on the landlord or agent managing the property.

No matter how diligent you have been the inspectors will always find something to improve.

Information Commissioner's Office

As a landlord you will in all probability be dealing with some information relating to tenants. Under the Data Protection Act anyone holding information must be registered with the Information Commission Office (ICO).

It is a simple process to become registered. Information on the registration process and fees can be found at http://www.ico.gov.uk/

You will receive a unique registration number and this must be renewed on an annual basis.

HMO (Housing of Multiple Occupation)

If you have a property that is a block of flats, student let or a house converted for a couple or several families to live in this is deemed an HMO. These HMO's must be registered with your local Council before you can let the property. You also have to be licensed with your local Council.

Fees and criteria for applications vary from Council to Council so it is best to contact your local Council and discuss their requirements.

Individual Houses

If you let a house to an unmarried couple with one child it can be deemed to be a house of multiple occupation i.e. there is more than one surname in the property. It could be that this house needs to be registered with the Council under HMO rules.

Each Council has different guidelines on what is an HMO and which HMO's need to be registered. Don't assume that as you have a traditional two storey family home that you are exempt. It is better to check with your local council than fall foul of the law. You can be prosecuted and face fines of up to £20,000.

If in doubt, check it out.

Advertising Your Property

There are various ways of advertising your property to let.

Councils

If you are an accredited landlord then using your local council website is free of charge. Provided you are prepared to accept tenants on benefits. You get free advertising to a large population.

Local Newspapers

Find out which night is their property to let night. Different papers run their property to let on different nights. My local runs their adverts on a Thursday night. I find it a waste of time placing the advert on any other night. The telephone never rings. If the advert is in on a Thursday night though, the phone rings on Thursday, Friday, Saturday and Sunday.

Online

When it comes to online advertising I found the best in my region at the moment is Gumtree. The telephone usually starts ringing within 2 hours of placing the ad. You can place 2 free ads per year and thereafter you need to pay for your adverts. I try to keep mine current by editing the ad on a weekly basis. If you want your ad to go to the top of the searches there is a small fee to pay. Play it by ear and see what works and what doesn't. No point spending money on advertising if you don't need to.

Window

I find the best form of advertising is placing your own sign in the window of the property to be let. I've had some simple signs made. They have black text on a white background. All that is on the boards is House to Let and the telephone number. The boards are the same size as a letting agent sign and for £100 I got 10 boards made. They are simple effective advertising and with large lettering can be easily read from the road.

Did you know that in Wales 40% of renters or buyers live close to their family. It is 28% in other parts of the country. With those statistics if you have a sign in your window the neighbours do the advertising for you.

Tenant Applications

Everyone has their own way of dealing with applications. My preference is to have a general meeting at the property and give the prospective tenants an application form to fill in.

I have a set application form and I request the following information:

- Full name of the applicant and any other adults who intend to live in the property
- Date of Birth
- National Insurance Number
- Previous address and if they have lived there for less than 3 years the address before that.
- Current Landlord, Address and Contact Number
- Employer
- Guarantor – plus date of birth and NI
- I ask for 2 written references to be attached to the application. One should be from their current landlord or employer. The other should be a character reference or reference from their bank, a lender or Hire Purchase company.
- A copy of their last 3 months bank statements
- Name and Address of a relative not living with them. This is used if a Bond is taken.

- There are a series of questions about having the bond and 1st months rent, do they have a criminal record, have they any CCJ's or court orders, have they been bankrupt, in arrears or evicted from another property.
- There is a declaration to sign agreeing to me making credit checks
- There is also a page of the key information from the tenancy agreement and they are signing to say they have read and accepted them.

Once I have all the information together I start the checks.

- Landlord Referencing Services – is an organisation for landlords to check with other landlords if the tenant has a good or bad record. There is no fee to join but you need to upload your existing tenants to the system and keep your records up to date.
- Write to the Employer for a Reference
- Do a credit check.
- If you have a guarantor, do exactly the same checks for them.

- Don't rush take you time and ensure you are happy before letting the property. Don't worry if the tenant is pushing to move in tomorrow. You need to do your checks and make sure you are entirely satisfied the applicant is right for you and your property. There is an old saying 'Marry in haste repent at leisure'. Well adapt that to read 'rent your property in haste and evict at leisure.

Guarantors

For most of my properties I request a guarantor. This is the person who is going to be responsible for paying the rent if the tenant fails.

In accepting someone to be a guarantor you need to be certain they can pay the rent if the tenant defaults. For this reason I do the same checks on the guarantor that I would do for a tenant.

Once I accept a guarantor then they are required to sign the tenancy along with the tenant. Their name is entered onto the tenancy as the guarantor and there is a separate section for them to sign.

Before signing the agreement I ensure they are aware that they must pay the rent in full if there is any default in the tenant paying the rent.

When signing the tenancy the guarantor must sign before the tenant for legal reasons. So there is no dispute on this I have a date and time section that the guarantor signs. I will then give the tenant some speech about the property, the tenancy etc. before getting them to sign date and time the agreement. This ensures there is a gap in time between the guarantor signing and the tenant signing.

I know some organisations prefer to get the guarantor to sign separate agreements. By getting the guarantor to sign the tenancy I also ensure the guarantor knows he is equally responsible for any problems during the tenancy.

Referencing

As part of the decision to let a property any potential tenants should be checked through referencing to ensure they are a suitable tenant. This will help to reduce the risk of bad debts.

Don't be afraid to ask for references and check them. The most common type of references are previous landlord, employer and character.

It is also common practice to ask for 3 months Bank Statements. This will show you if the tenant has had any problems with bounced cheques or direct debits and helps you to also judge if the tenant can afford the rent.

Landlord Referencing Service

Landlord Referencing Service is a free online service available to landlords. It is set up and operated by landlords for landlords. The principal behind the system is that a database is held of landlords and tenants. When a landlord asks for a tenant search they are provided with details of a previous landlord. Both landlords then talk to each other about the prospective tenant.

For the system to work landlords need to keep the information on their tenants up to date. I once received a call from a landlord asking for a reference on an existing tenant. I was unaware the tenant was looking for alternative accommodation. The landlord informed the tenant they needed to let us know and provide notice if or when they were intending to leave. Communication between us and the Landlord worked well. We were given plenty of notice the tenant was leaving. He knew he was getting a good tenant.

Experian

Landlord Referencing Service has a joint venture with Experian Credit Search. For a discount you can obtain a written report about the prospective tenant and their credit history. It is recommended that every landlord do a credit search on each prospective tenant.

From the credit search you can see if the prospective tenant has any financial problems. You can also see how often they move. Are you looking for a long term tenant or a tenant that is only going to be with you for a few months?

Employer

Just because the prospective tenant says they are employed doesn't mean they are. Check with employers and see if the prospective tenant has a good employment record. Are they likely to lose their job or stay employed for the foreseeable future? I've been caught out once where I didn't check with an employer and the month after I had granted a tenancy the tenant informed me he was now unemployed, couldn't pay the rent and was waiting for housing benefit to be sorted before he could pay me. Three months later housing benefit informed me the tenant was only entitled to £18 per week. I then had to deal with a bad debt, a tenant eviction and could have saved myself some stress and expense if only I had checked the stability of employment for the tenant.

Insurance

Insurance is covered under a separate section but if you are looking for rent guarantee insurance you will need to provide suitable referencing for the prospective tenant.

Insurance

In addition to buildings insurance on your property you can get a rent guarantee insurance. If the tenant defaults on payments you are protected against not receiving rent during the period. With the economic conditions in 2012 it is good business practice to have the insurance in place.

The cost is around £100 for a year and while this is a reasonable amount to pay if you have a defaulting tenant your losses can add up to far more than this in a very short time. As a landlord you will probably have a mortgage on the property and it is very important to ensure you can pay the mortgage even if the tenant is not paying you.

There are numerous companies offering this service. Check out the small print though and make sure you comply with all the terms and conditions. Insurance companies are notorious for finding a loophole to get out of paying.

Tenancy Agreements

A tenancy agreement is an arrangement between the landlord and tenant to let a property for a certain period of time under certain conditions. The contract can be verbal or written. In practise it is better in writing as then there can be no dispute over the terms and conditions.

In practise a written tenancy agreement is called an Assured Shorthold Tenancy. It sets out the term the landlord agrees to let the property for. Usually, around 6 months but can be for anything from 1 day to several years. For this example we'll assume a standard 6 month tenancy.

The Assured Shorthold Tenancy (AST) will have a fixed period of 6 months commencing on a specific date and ending 6 months later. After, this time the tenancy becomes a periodic tenancy and continues on a month by month basis until cancelled either by the tenant leaving the property or by a new tenancy agreement being put in place.

Ending The AST

Either the landlord or the tenant can end the tenancy by giving the correct notice period. This is often misunderstood by both the landlord and the tenant.

The landlord must give the tenant two full tenancy months notice to leave the property. i.e. the tenancy start date is the 14th of the month. The tenant must receive in writing notice that the landlord wants the property back before the 14th of the month. For this example we will assume it is June. The tenant must receive the notice before the 14th June. The tenant would be asked to leave the property by 13th August thus giving two full tenancy months notice.

If the tenancy is still in a fixed term then the notice would be for the end of the fixed term but still requires a minimum two tenancy months notice.

The tenant must provide the landlord with one month's notice in writing that they are terminating the agreement. Using the example above the tenant would need to notify the landlord before the 14th July that they are leaving on the 13th August. If the landlord receives the notice on or after the 14th July, the tenant would not legally be permitted to leave the property until the 13th September. If the tenant left the property on the

13th August the landlord would be entitled to charge the tenant for rent up to the 13th September as full and proper notice had not been received.

Other Terms and Conditions

The landlord has the responsibility to maintain the exterior of the property. i.e. the Walls, Roof, Front Door and the Exterior Drains. These items cannot be written out of an agreement. The only way for the landlord to get out of this clause is through a court order and that is normally only granted on mental grounds.

The landlord also has to ensure there is heating and hot available in the property otherwise all interior maintenance and gardens are the responsibility of the tenant and should be written into the tenancy agreement so the tenant is made aware of their responsibilities.

Where the landlord provides electrical equipment such as ovens, fridges etc. the landlord should ensure the tenant is made aware that if a fault occurs the tenant is responsible for repairs or replacement of a similar item.

There is a legal term referred to as 'tenant like manner' which means the tenant should treat the property as though it were their own property and maintain it accordingly. This is often overlooked with many tenants assuming the landlord should be running around after them. Having tenant responsibilities written into the tenancy agreement will help to alleviate this concept.

Who Is The Tenant?

Any adult living in the property is deemed to be the tenant. It is therefore important that all adults are named on the tenancy agreement. If you are aware a person is living in the property but not on the tenancy it could be deemed that the person concerned has a verbal tenancy with the landlord. This then makes it difficult to prove a tenancy exists and to later evict the tenant. Therefore always make sure every adult living in the property is named on a written tenancy agreement.

How Much Information Do You Put in A Tenancy Agreement?

The answer is as much information as is needed to ensure the tenant is aware of their obligations. Also whatever is needed to protect you the landlord.

A colleague of mine with a large portfolio of properties has 67 pages in his tenancy agreement. I have 12 pages in mine. Early in 2012 I did some work with the Welsh Assembly on setting up a standard tenancy agreement for Wales and the proposal was for 25 pages of terms and conditions. I know some landlords who have a one or two page tenancy agreement.

Don't be afraid to write a novel when putting an agreement together. The more information in the agreements the less chance the tenant can say they did not know something. The more protection there is for the landlord should difficulties arise.

Lawpack produce tenancy agreements which can be purchased from shops such as WH Smith or Staples. They are okay to get you started. I used these when I first started renting properties in 2001. As problems arose I added more terms and conditions to the extent that I now have 12 pages in the tenancy agreement.

Rents

Once of the biggest questions I get asked is how do you know much rent to charge?

First, I walk around the letting agents and get an idea of how much properties are renting for in the area. I use this as a guide line only. Many Estate Agents, who are managing properties will try and force the price down to give them a wider scope for applicants. I then work out what I need to cover the mortgage, legalities etc. and set a price from there.

In early 2012, I was approached by one Estate Agent to manage my properties. I am not keen on Agents but did say I was willing for them to find a tenant for me. The Agent viewed the property and asked how much I wanted for it. My response was £600 per calendar month (pcm). The agent sent along 2 couples totally unsuitable for the property then stated the rent was too high and I should drop it to around £500 pcm. My response is not printable in this book. I put the rent up to £650 pcm and within a week the property was let to a couple who said they would have been happy to pay up to £1000 for such a lovely property. They have been renting it for almost a year and are a lovely couple who look after the place and pay their rent on time.

Setting rents really is a personal decision. I tend to stay near the top of the range for properties in the area that way I attract a better client. Be flexible though and be prepared to negotiate if you think you have the right tenant.

If your property doesn't let then you may have to consider a lower rent and advertise accordingly or do like I did and put the rent up.

I remember reading a story about Donald Trump. He built an apartment block in New York and the apartments weren't selling. He was advised to drop the price to attract more interest. Instead, he put up the asking price by an enormous sum so each apartment was over a million dollars to buy. Within months he had sold all the apartments. The perception was the apartments had more value because the price was higher. It is amazing how often I have applied this concept to setting rents if a property isn't moving.

Frequency

Rents are generally charged per calendar month and payable in advance. This can cause problems if you take on benefit tenants who receive their benefit on a 4 weekly basis in arrears. Again, you will need to be flexible based on the type of tenant you want in the property.

Weekly rents

It is possible to charge rents on a weekly basis. However, it is a legal requirement that where rents are charged on a weekly basis the tenant must be given a rent book. The book must be updated each time rent is paid.

Paying Rent

You decide how you want the rent paid. It might be that you want to collect it on the due date each month. My preference is for the tenant to pay the rent direct to my bank account. I write this into the tenancy agreement and provide them with bank details and the reference I want to show on the tenancy. I use the property address as the reference because with a large portfolio you'd be amazed how many G Jones I have as tenants. It is easier to match a property reference than a name reference.

Rent Reviews

You should have a rent review built into your tenancy agreement on an annual basis. I use the CPI figure on which to base my rent increases. If the rents appear to be going up quite quickly I will only increase an existing rent by a small amount. If the tenant is good I don't want to upset them by increasing rents by large amounts.

Rents can only be increased legally once a year. So ensure you have sufficient margin built into your rents if mortgage interest rates start increasing. You could find yourself out of pocket if mortgages go up too much. Don't assume that because Bank of England Base Rate is low your mortgage interest rate will stay low. I have some lenders who put up their interest rate on an annual basis.

Bonds/Deposits

There is a law that requires any bonds or deposits to be registered with a Government Approved Bond Scheme. There are 3 such schemes.

Deposit Protection Service

This is a free custodial service where you give Deposit Protect Services the money you have received from the tenant. They hold the money until the tenancy ends and the deposit is returned to the tenant in full or less any claim you have for rent default or property damage.

Tenancy Deposit scheme

This is an insurance based scheme and the deposit is only paid to TDS if there is a dispute. They then hold the full deposit until such time as the dispute is settled. Discounts are available on the fees for members of Residential Landlords Organisation.

MyDeposits

This is also an insurance based scheme where the landlord takes out an insurance cover to protect the deposit. It operates the same way TDS does. There are discounts for members of the National Landlord Association.

Adjudication

With all the schemes there is an independent adjudication service which assesses any dispute between the tenant and landlord over withholding any part of the deposit when it is due to be returned to the tenant at the end of the tenancy.

Legal Requirments

1. Landlords are required to register the bond with one of the above services within 30 days of taking the bond from the tenant. Failure to do so can result in you receiving a hefty fine of having to pay the tenant up to 3 times more than the deposit and you can lose your right to evict the tenant.

2. You need to give the tenant prescribed information when securing the deposit. The information to be supplied is:
    a. the address of the rented property
    b. how much deposit you've paid
    c. how the deposit is protected
    d. the name and contact details of the TDP scheme and its dispute resolution service
    e. the landlord (or the letting agency's) name and contact details
    f. the name and contact details of any third party that's paid the deposit
    g. why the landlord would keep some or all of the deposit
    h. how to apply to get the deposit back
    i. what to do if you can't get hold of the landlord at the end of the tenancy
    j. what to do if there's a dispute over the deposit

Cautions

- Don't make the mistake of saying I don't take a bond I ask for 2 months rent up front. This is the same as taking a deposit and one month's rent must be secured under a tenancy deposit scheme.

- If you take money to hold a property it doesn't become a deposit until the tenancy is signed. It must then be secured under a tenancy deposit scheme within 30 days.
- Prescribed Information – this is the information you must provide to the tenant as detailed above. You must provide the tenant with all the information details above. If you do not write to the tenant with the prescribed information you may be liable to the penalties as if you did not secure the deposit. This is a grey area at present as the government have allowed claims for not supplying the prescribed information to be back dated 6 years to when tenancy deposits initially started. At the moment the legal profession are waiting for test cases to go to court. This could result in companies targeting tenants to see if they can get any money back similar to the current PPI banking claims.

Inventories

There is currently no legal requirement to do an inventory of the rental property. It is just good business practice to do so.

An inventory provides the landlord and the tenant with a reference point against which to measure if any damage has been done to the property or not. Relying on memory doesn't work.

You can make an inventory as simple or as complicated as you want. It could be a simple one page document that describes the condition of the property or it can be a detailed report of every room in the property describing the walls, ceilings and flooring along with pictures.

The more information you put into the inventory the easier it will be to compare the condition of the property during and at the end of the tenancy. It is important that you allow for normal wear and tear during the tenancy but generally speaking the property should be in the same condition when you get it back as it was at the start of the tenancy.

There are extremes of tenants from an exceptional tenant to the worst tenant possible. I've had them all and you probably will in your rental property business. My best tenant rented 3 different properties from me. Each time they painted the interior from top to bottom. They even had the carpets cleaned on an annual basis. This couple were tenants for 11 years before the husband died and the wife went to live with her family. They were such fantastic tenants they became friends.

On the other hand, I've also had tenants from hell. They systematically demolished the interior of the property removing interior doors, flooring and even the toilet seats. When I tried to evict them they obtained legal aid and then tried to sue me for disrepair of the property. Luckily, I had an inventory done by an independent company which showed the property was in good condition when they moved in. They lost their case but not until I had spent a small fortune defending it. If there hadn't been an inventory I could have lost the court case and would probably had to pay another £30,000 - £50,000 in court costs and legal fees.

So, as I said earlier, it makes good business sense to have an inventory for a property that is being let.

Property Manuals

Another tool I have found useful but again is not a legal requirement is to have a property manual. For this I use a simple ring binder and I update the information each time I visit the property.

In each manual I provide the following information:

- Property Address and Post Code
- Details of Local Council
- Property Management Details
- Energy Performance Certificate
- Gas Safety Certificate
- NICEIC Certificate
- The Inventory
- A log of visits made to the property

This information is useful if you are in dispute with the tenant on maintenance or other issues as there is a ready log available for each visit. I get the tenant to sign the log along with my signature. If the tenant raises any issues the matters are recorded in the log. I also take a photograph of the log on my smart phone and keep the record in the office. This might seem extreme but when you have dealt with as many scams as I have over the past decade or so then you will understand the importance of good records.

An acquaintance of mine carries a tape recorder in his pocket and records all conversations with tenants. At the end of each day he downloads the information to his computer. A permanent record of conversations.

HMO

HMO stands for House of Multiple Occupation. Sometimes defining what is a house of multiple occupation can be more difficult.

The most common types of HMO's are flats, student lets and houses that have been converted into rentals that can be used by more than one family. In each case the property and the landlord must be registered with the local council before the property can be let. There are also some additional compliances required at the property and the local council will advise you on those. These relate to safety compliances and information that must be displayed in the property.

Sometimes it is more difficult to realise you have a HMO. For instance, if you let a property to an unmarried couple who then have a child the property could be classed as an HMO. This is because there are two or more surnames using the property. However, the same property if let to a married couple with a child is purely a family home. The same property under the law can be classed as a family home or a HMO.

The best thing to do to ensure you do not fall foul of local council laws is to find out from the council what definition they use for a HMO and which type of HMO they require you to register with them. It is better to be safe than sorry. There are hefty penalties if you do not comply with the regulations.

Bad Debts

It doesn't matter how many checks you do on prospective tenants eventually you will come across a tenant who doesn't pay their rent. Prompt management of the situation is important so the matter does not get out of control.

Here are some of the measures I use:

- Contact the tenant by phone the next day and find out why they have not paid
- Follow up in writing within 5 days if the rent has still not been received. Let the tenant know they are incurring penalties for late payment
- If rent still not received within 14 days refer the tenant to the terms and conditions in the tenancy agreement stating I have the right to evict them for non payment of rent where it is 14 days overdue
- Issue Section 21 notice and advise tenant they can still stay in the property provided the rent is paid in full and all future payments are made on time.
- If the tenant still doesn't pay commence eviction proceedings

- Contact local council to see if the tenant has any LHA (formerly Housing Benefit) entitlement and ask for future payments to be made direct to landlord
- Update tenant information on Landlord Referencing
- File outstanding rent plus costs with Court and obtain CCJ.

From experience if you let a situation go on for just a few more days it can quickly get out of control and you are facing rent arrears of £3000, £5000 or more before the tenant is evicted and repossession of the property is granted.

Section 8 and Section 21 Notices

Rent arrears is the most common reason for a landlord to evict a tenant but do you use a Section 8 notice or a Section 21 notice?

A Section 8 notice is served on a tenant when the tenant is a minimum of two months in arrears. Normally, the grounds (reasons) for serving the notice are Grounds 8, 10 and 11. This states the tenant is in arrears, has continual arrears and is late making payments. The tenant has a period of 14 days to pay the rent or be taken to court. If rent is not paid an application is made for a court hearing. The date for the hearing is set at the court's convenience and usually takes two to three months for the date to be set.

It seems an easy process, attend court and get the property returned to the landlord, but once in court the Section 8 notice can be defended. It is becoming more common for the tenant to defend a Section 8 notice with the assistance of legal aid.

During the hearing or just before the hearing the tenant can pay just enough money to bring the amount owed to one pound under the two months arrears and the case is thrown out of court. The whole eviction process starts again.

Another defence being used is the tenant can claim disrepair of the property. Further court hearings are set while independent inspections of the property are made. This can then escalate to a court trial. Legal costs are high and if the landlord loses the case he has to pay court costs and legal aid costs for the tenant along with his own solicitor fees. It is not uncommon for landlords to be facing bills of twenty or thirty thousand pounds.

The alternative to a Section 8 notice is a Section 21 notice.

With a Section 21 the landlord serves the notice on the tenant stating the landlord wants possession of the property on a specific date. The landlord needs an independent witness who can verify the notice was served correctly. The Section 21 must give the tenant two full tenancy months notice to leave the property. If the tenant does not leave on the due date the landlord files an application with the court for possession of the property. The court allows the tenant 14 days to respond. Without anyone attending court the judge makes a decision on the date possession is given to the landlord, usually within 14 days provided the landlord has proven delivery of the Section 21 notice, correct notice dates were used and the landlord has complied with legislation relating to any bonds or deposits taken. The only defence the tenant can use is requiring more time to leave the property. It is then at the judge's discretion where to order the tenant to leave in 14 days or 28 days.

Section 8 notices used to be the favoured way of evicting a tenant for rent arrears as it was suppose to be the quickest way to obtain repossession of a property. Today with the stresses on the court system dates it often takes two or three months to get a hearing date. If the tenant defends the notice time can be dragged out to a year or longer. Using a Section 21 notice takes three to four months to evict the tenant. The landlord does not give a reason for the notice only stating the landlord wants the property back. If the landlord wishes to pursue the tenant for rent arrears once possession of the property has been returned to the landlord this can be done through the small claims court or money online system. The landlord can make a claim up to six months after the tenant has left the property.

A Section 21 Notice

When issuing a Section 21 notice there is no prescribed format. A simple letter asking the tenant to give you back possession of the property on a specific date is all that is required. The dates need to link in to the tenancy agreement and provide the full notice period.

The format I use is on the next page:

NOTICE REQUIRING POSSESSION

(Housing Act 1988, Section 21)

ENGLAND & WALES

To: **Tenant Name and Address**

From: **Landlord Name and Address**

I give you notice that, by virtue of Section 21 of the Housing Act 1988, I require possession of the dwelling known as: (Rental Property Address)

After: **(last date of tenancy period two months after date notice issued)** or after the last day of the period of your tenancy which expires next after the end of two months from the date of service of this notice to you.

Signed: **Landlord Signature**

Name: **Landlord Name**

Date: **date notice issued**

Court

As my personal preference is for Section 21 notice the court proceedings stated below relate to Section 21 Notices.

If the tenant fails to leave the property by the due date the landlord must ask the court to give the landlord possession of the property. This is done by completing a court form N5B and paying the appropriate fee to the court. The form is available to download from the court website.

When delivering the form N5B to the court there needs to be several copies attached - one copy for each of the tenants so if there are two tenants there needs to be two copies. The court will also want a copy for their records. I also keep a copy for my own records.

At the time of writing this in 2012 the fee is £175.00 as the fee does change check with the court for the current fee. You will also need to check with the court which court is responsible for the rental property concerned. The form N5B and supporting documents need to go to that court.

Once the court receives the forms they issue notice to the tenant. The tenant has 14 days to respond. The landlord receives a notice from the court telling them when the notice period is up and when they can ask for a judgement.

Once the notice period is over send in the slip asking for a judgement and the landlord should receive the repossession order within a few days with the date the property goes back to the landlord.

If the tenant responds to the notice the judge will make an order without the landlord sending back the slip asking for judgement.

Court Bailiff

Once the landlord has obtained an order from the court for repossession of the property often the tenant still does not leave the property. In these circumstances the landlord has to apply to the court for a bailiff to be appointed to evict the tenant.

Using the court forms download the request for bailiff form and send to the court along with the appropriate fee. The current fee is £110.00. The court will then appoint a bailiff.

This process is slow and it can take a few months to get a date with the bailiff to attend the property.

One week before the date the bailiff will visit the property and advise the tenant they must leave before the set date. On the given date the landlord meets the bailiff at the property. The bailiff will check the tenant is not in the property and ask the landlord to change the locks. If the tenant then returns and enters the property they can be charged with trespass.

If the tenant is still in the property the bailiff will give them about 10 minutes to leave and if the tenant still fails to go the bailiff will ask for the police to attend the property and arrest the tenant for failing to comply with a court order.

County Court Judgements (CCJ)

If a tenant has left the landlord's property with rent arrears, damage to the property or outstanding bills the landlord can apply to the court for a County Court Judgement (CCJ). Once a CCJ has been obtained if the ex-tenant is working the landlord can apply for an enforcement order against wages until the debt is paid.

How to Apply for A County Court Judgement (CCJ)

The easiest way to apply for a CCJ is through the court online system at https://www.moneyclaim.gov.uk the landlord will need to open an account. Once done all applications for money owing to the landlord can be done through this website. It will take you step by step through the process. If the landlord doesn't have a forwarding address for the tenant then the court documents can be served at the tenants last known address i.e. the rental property.

The usual process is:

- The landlord completes online application
- The tenant is given 28 days to respond.
- If no response landlord asks for judgement.

- If the tenant responds the judge can suggest arbitration
- If there is no arbitration or arbitration is unsuccessful a date is set for the landlord and tenant to present their points of view to the judge. There are no lawyers involved.
- The CCJ remains on the tenants credit history for 6 years.

Court Costs

There is a cost to use this service and it is pro-rata on the amount being claimed. Costs are added to the judgement.

Many landlords decide the costs and time involved in this process are not worth the landlord's time. However, I would encourage every landlord who has a debt to use the service. You do not know what the tenant will do in the future and some landlords have received money five or six years down the track. It is also beneficial for other landlords when doing credit referencing to know if there is a debt against a prospective tenant.

Section 2 Summary

This section has outlined some of the finer points of being a landlord. No business is perfect and most incur their fair share of problems. But rental properties offer the investor a good return for the investment, on going income and potential for capital growth.

As with any investment it is best to read as much as you can about the type of investment you chose.

If being a 'hands on' landlord is not for you then there are many agents who will manage the property for you. Again research the agent as most are poor and some are just above that level. I have yet to find an outstanding agent providing good service to both the landlord and the tenant. At the first sign of trouble many will hand the problem back to the landlord to deal with. Research carefully which agents you use.

Tiroka Property Management Services

I am not a fan of letting agents as I have found too often the service provided by the company fell far short of what was promised. Agent fees were often very high for the service being provided. Where I have used letting agents they have always let me down. For this reason I set up my own property management company. The company provides the services and systems that meet my needs. I think of it as a management company design by a landlord for landlords.

While Tiroka Property Management Services does some lettings the main function of the business is to provide admin support services to landlords. These services include tenant referencing; tenancy agreements; inventories, property compliances and all services needed to evict a tenant including serving Section 21 notices.

Each of the services is stand alone product so the landlord does not have to use a specific service to access any of the other services. Landlords who want to manage their own properties can do so and use Tiroka Property Management Services like their own personal assistant to provide the admin services the landlord is unsure of or just doesn't want to get involved with.

More information is available at:

Website: www.tirokapms.co.uk

Email: admin@tirokapms.co.uk

Telephone: 0845 337 0559

Recommended Reading

Rich Dad, Poor Dad – Robert Kiyosaki

Cashflow Quadrant – Robert Kiyosaki

Rich Dad's Guide to Investing – Robert Kiyosaki

Rich Dad Prophecy – Robert Kiyosaki

Increase Your Financial IQ – Robert Kiyosaki

Who took my money – Robert Kiyosaki

Guide to Becoming Rich – Robert Kiyosaki

The Business School – Robert Kiyosaki

Conspiracy of the Rich – Robert Kiyosaki

Unfair Advantage – Robert Kiyosaki

The Real Book of Real Estate – Robert Kiyosaki

Real Estate Riches – Dolf de Roos

The Compound Effect – Darren Hardy

The Instant Millionaire – Mark Fisher

Secrets of the Millionaire Mind – T Harv Eker

Other Books By Karen Newton

On the following pages you will find details of other books available from Karen Newton.

Beginners Guide To The Sharemarket

A beginner's guide to the sharemarket is a simple step by step to investing in shares.

Karen explains her two strategies of investing for high yield dividends and capital growth through undervalued companies or penny share companies.

Understand the power of compound interest through the story of the fairy godmother and the magic train and you will think twice about how simple it really is to acquire great wealth.

This book is out of general print but available in a digital version. For further information email info@karennewton.co.uk or visit the website www.karennewton.co.uk

29 Hours A Day

Have you ever wondered why some people seem to do so much during the day while you struggle with your workload.

29 hours a day shows you simple techniques to improve your time management skills and achieve more in a day than you thought possible.

This book is out of general print but is available in a digital version. For further information email <info@karennewton.co.uk> or visit the website <www.karennewton.co.uk>

Insider Guide to Investing in Art

Rembrandt, Monet and Picasso are some of the worlds best know artists. Today their paintings are worth millions. Yet, they started their careers with little or no money needing supporters to help them survive from day to day.

Insider Guide to Investing in Art will help you identify the artists of today who are likely to be the successes of tomorrow. Buy their art today and it could be worth millions tomorrow.

This book is out of general print but available in a digital version. For further information email info@karennewton.co.uk or visit the website www.karennewton.co.uk

Niche – A Guide To Niche Marketing

Imagine having a ready made customer base all eager to buy your product.

This beginners guide to Niche Marketing explains where and how to find customers what to sell to the customer and more importantly how to sell to them. Then once you have captured your audience how to continually sell more profitable items to them.

This book is due for release in 2013 in both digital and paperback versions through Amazon Books.

Surviving 2013 – A Financial Guide

Surviving 2013 is a guide to financial education covering the skills and knowledge needed to build an income producing portfolio.

Karen describes her financial pyramid for ensuring a strong financial base, security, growth and income. Discover how simple steps can help your create financial independence.

Find out how invest £2.73 a day could make you a millionaire and discover how Karen borrowed £300 on a credit card and turned it into £10 million.

This book is available through numerous outlets and online including Amazon Books.

www.ingramcontent.com/pod-product-compliance
Lightning Source LLC
Chambersburg PA
CBHW061511180526
45171CB00001B/131